McFarland

# South Pacific Seafarers

## A. G. Smith

DOVER PUBLICATIONS, INC.
Mineola, New York

# South Pacific Seafarers

When European explorers first encountered the island groups scattered across the Pacific Ocean they found them populated with well-developed societies. The inhabitants of these islands, thousands of miles from the continents of Asia and the Americas, were, not surprisingly, masters of the skills of navigation. Beginning around 2500 B.C., these ancestors of the modern Micronesians, Melanesians, and Polynesians had spread out from the large islands off the coast of Southeast Asia (Java, Sumatra, New Guinea) across the Pacific.

When forced to seek new homes because of famine, overpopulation, or defeat in war, these seafaring people would prepare to migrate. They constructed large double-hulled canoes that could carry forty or more people, and their livestock, for voyages of several months. The largest of these craft could sail more than 150 miles a day. Their navigators knew the seasonal positions of all the major stars and constellations. They had also learned to recognize wave patterns and currents as well as such signs as migrating birds and cloud formations near land.

On arrival at a suitable uninhabited island, the new settlers would begin to adapt themselves and their way of life to the new environment. They also adapted their boat designs and building techniques to the local conditions and available materials.

Over the centuries, this migration and adaptation process was repeated numerous times. By A.D. 700 almost all the habitable islands in the Pacific, as far east as the coast of South America, had been populated.

The knowledge and techniques of these early seafarers continue to be studied today. The astounding skill and courage of these master navigators inspire the respect of all modern sailors, and the imaginations of armchair adventurers everywhere.

A. G. SMITH

Marshall Islands "stick charts." The sticks represent wave patterns and ocean currents; the cowrie shells, island groups.

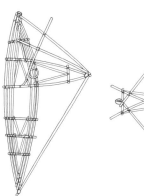 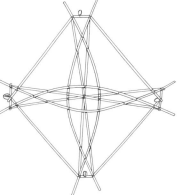

*Copyright*

*Bibliographical Note*

*South Pacific Seafarers* is a new work, first published by Dover Publications, Inc., in 2003.

DOVER *Pictorial Archive* SERIES

*International Standard Book Number: 0-486-42380-8*

Manufactured in the United States of America
Dover Publications, Inc., 31 East 2nd Street, Mineola, N.Y. 11501

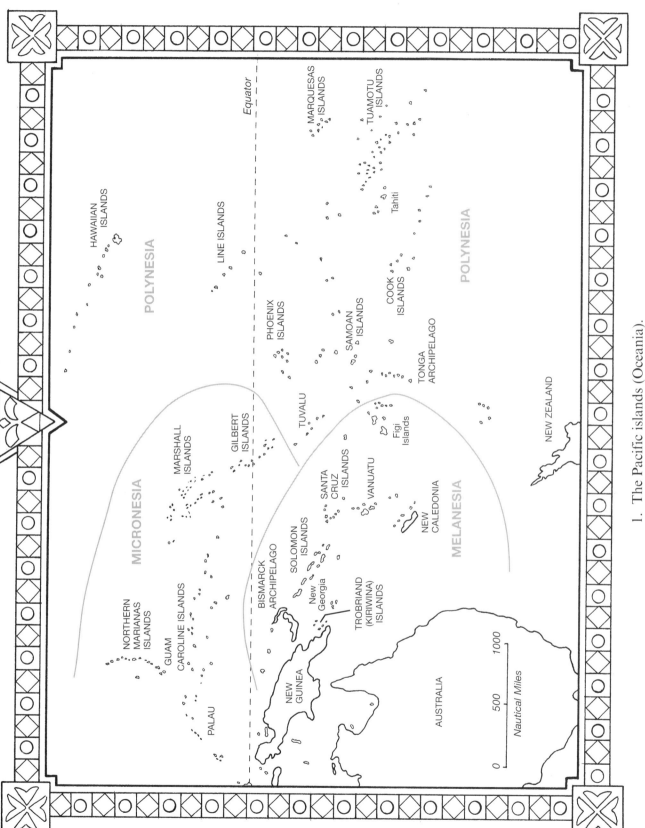

1. The Pacific islands (Oceania).

2. A log dugout ("paopao") with single outrigger, Tonga Archipelago.

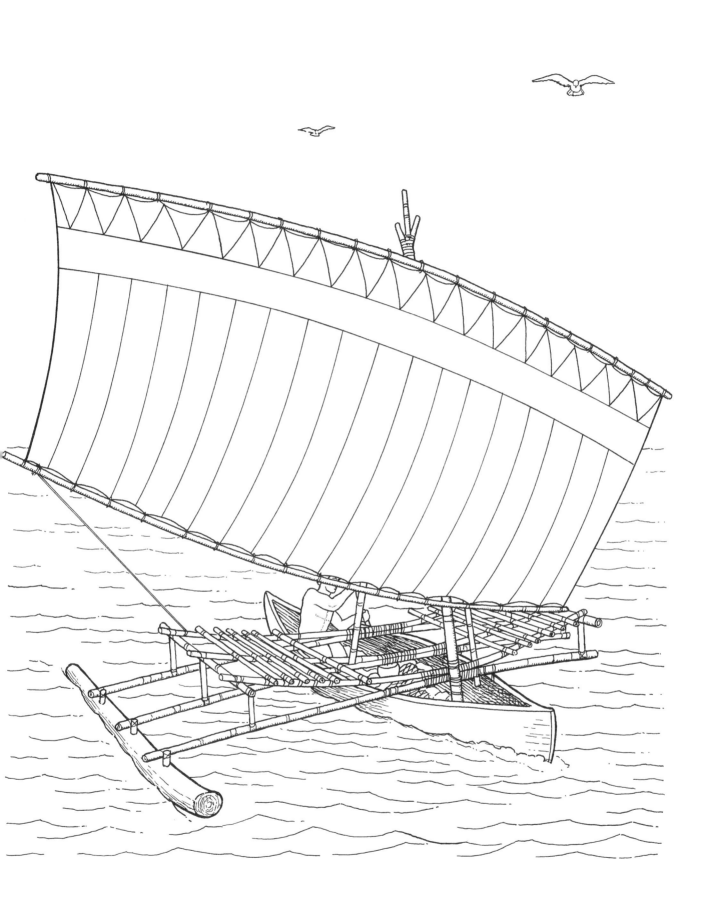

3. A Moro outrigger, Philippines.

4. Carving a dugout canoe, Fiji Islands.

5. Canoes were treated with fire to harden them and inhibit deterioration.

6. The seaworthiness of the narrow carved hulls of small canoes was greatly enhanced by the attachment of lightweight outrigger floats. Each island group had its own special techniques for attaching the booms and stanchions to the floats.

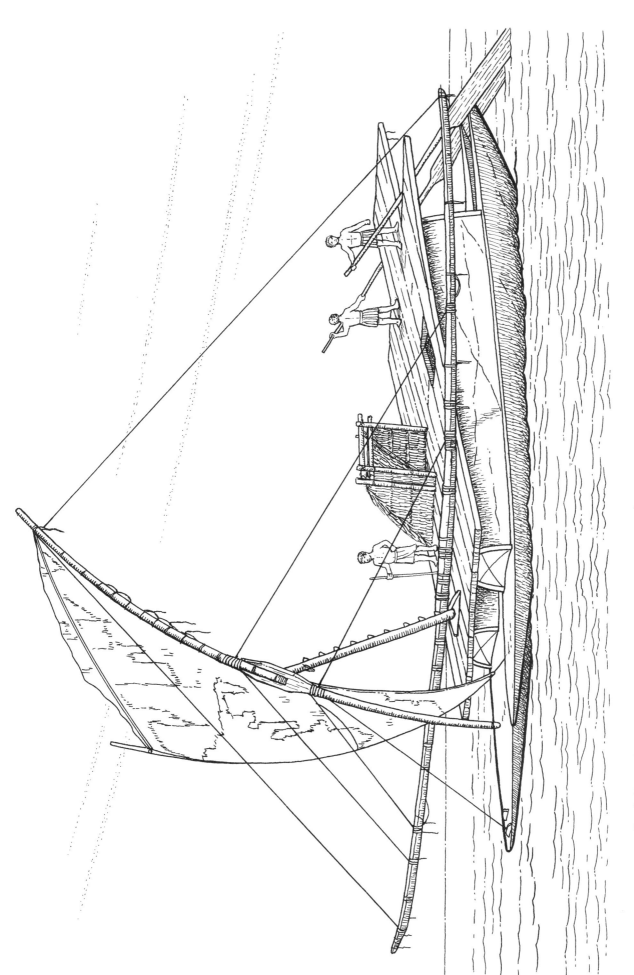

7. A "Tongiaki" double canoe, Tonga Archipelago. Large double canoes were the type used for migration. Some could carry as many as 40 or 50 people.

8. In addition to woodworking and shipbuilding skills, other crafts were needed for seafaring. The man on the upper right is pounding plant fibers to soften them. The woman in the center is weaving a mat for a sail panel. The young man on the lower right is braiding twisted plant fiber into rope.

9. A war canoe and boathouse, New Georgia, Solomon Islands. Note the slits in the matting on the front of the boathouse to allow for the passage of the high stem and stern of the canoe.

10. Turtle fishermen tying a captured animal to an outrigger.

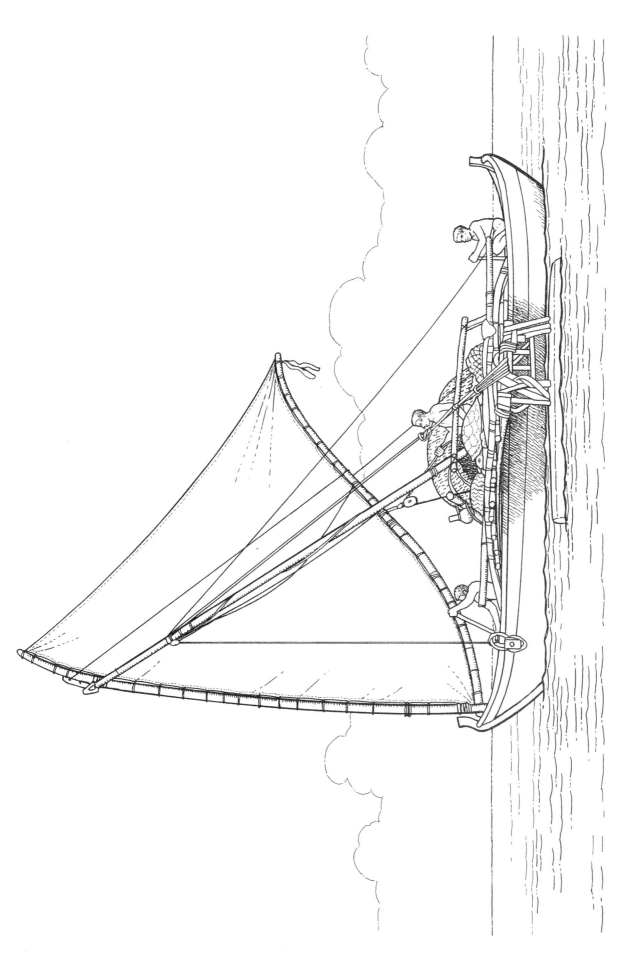

11. A Gilbert Islands sailing outrigger with a turtle tied to the boom platform. The mast is raked sharply forward.

12. An outrigger canoe, Nui, Tuvalu.

13. A Marshall Islands sailing canoe. The Marshall Islanders were noted for their excellent boatbuilding and navigation skills.

14. The Maori of New Zealand were a proud warrior society. They developed war canoes for raids on other island communities. When Captain Cook arrived in the 1770s they showed no curiosity or desire to trade and attempted to drive the Europeans away.

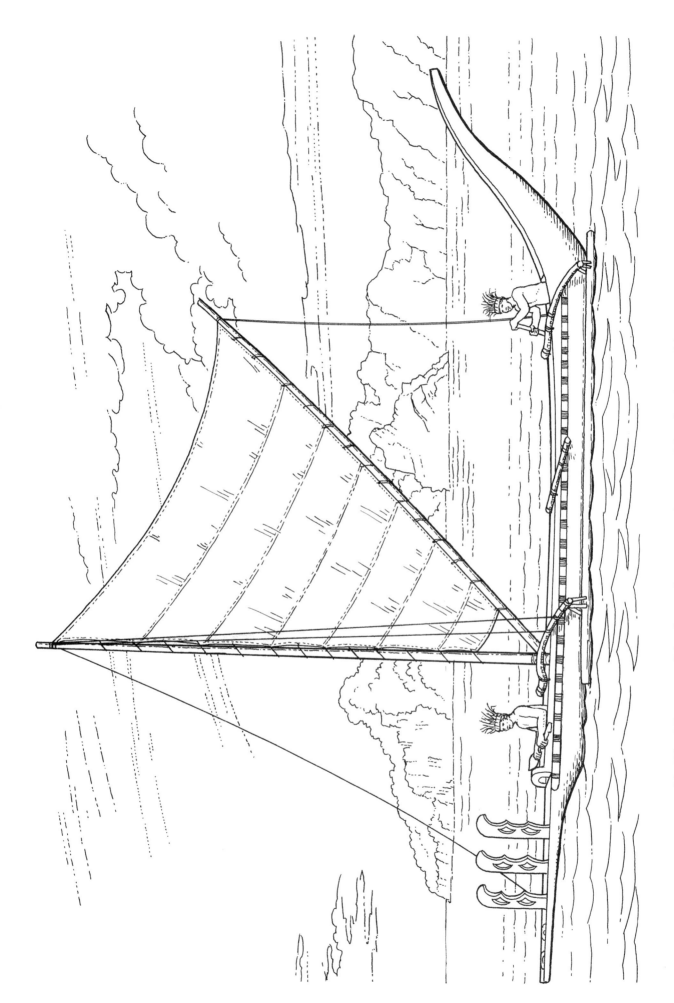

15. The Marquesas Islands outrigger canoe is unusual for the shape of its upswept stern.

16. Some seagoing canoes were steered by turning a steering paddle with a tiller attached. Others such as the sailing canoe of the Ninigo Islands, Bismarck Archipelago, were steered by raising and lowering the steering paddle vertically.

17. A fifty-foot ocean sailing canoe with outrigger, Luf Islands, Bismarck Archipelago. The hull is covered with patterned decoration.

18. A Trobriand (Kiriwina) Islands sailing canoe ("masawa"). The sail is made from large tough leaves sewn together.

19. Canoe figureheads represented gods or spirits and gave luck to the crew.
Top: Polynesia, possibly Maori. Bottom: New Georgia, Solomon Islands.

20.  Children were taught to handle small boats from a very early age.

21. A master navigator teaching navigation using a "stone canoe," Gilbert Islands. The triangular stones represent ocean swells' angle and size.

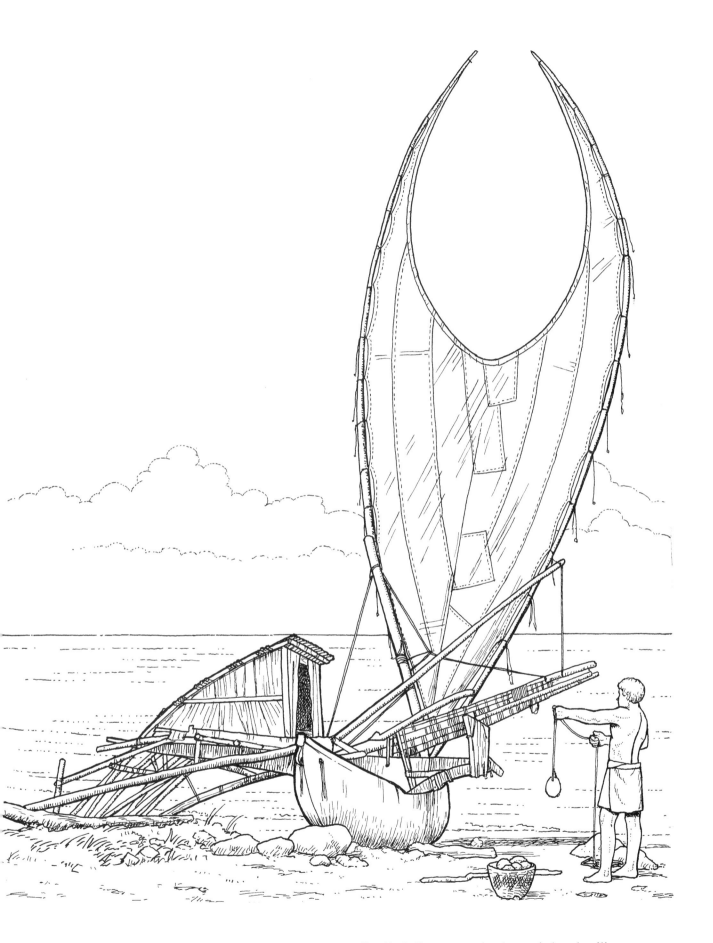

22. A Santa Cruz Islands outrigger with "crab claw" sail. Sail types evolved to suit local sailing conditions and available materials.

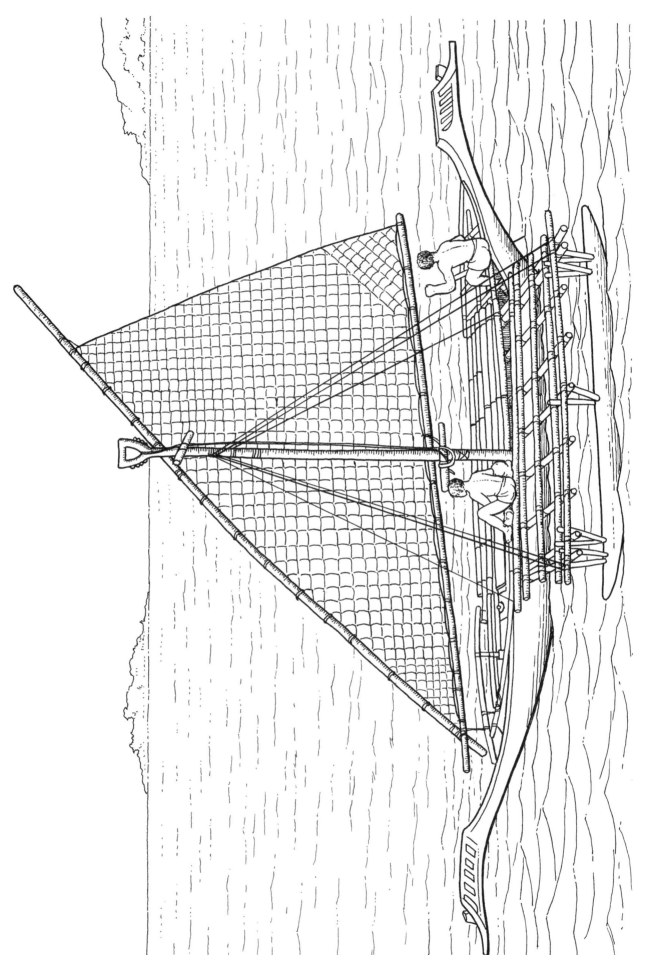

23. A sailing canoe with woven mat lateen sail, Takutea, Cook Islands.

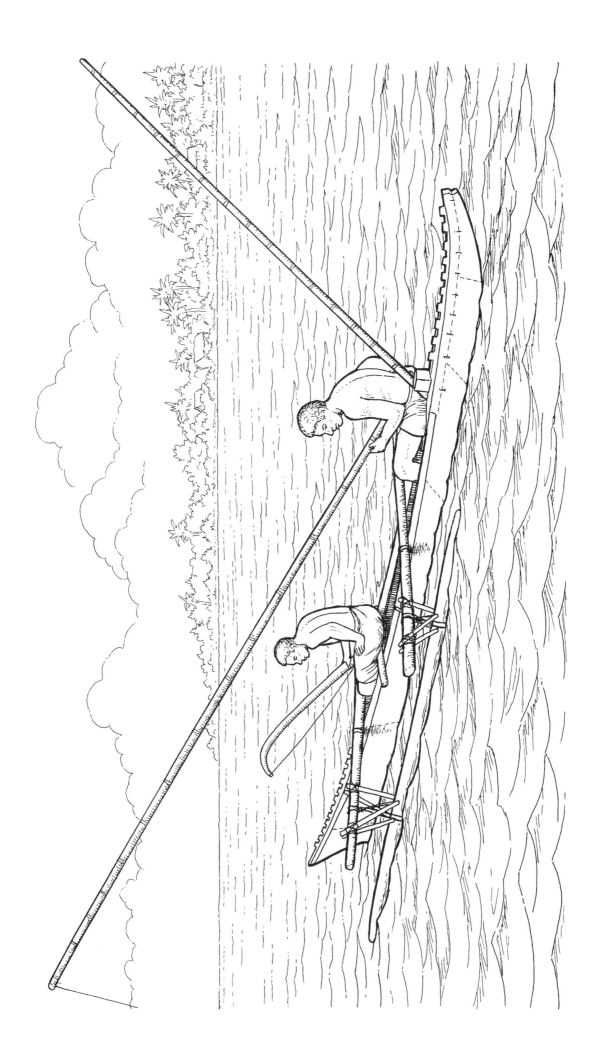

24. Fishing for bonito (tuna) from an outrigger canoe, Samoan Islands.

25. Fishing in the Solomon Islands. Fishermen surrounded schools of fish with nets and then used spears to bring them into canoes.

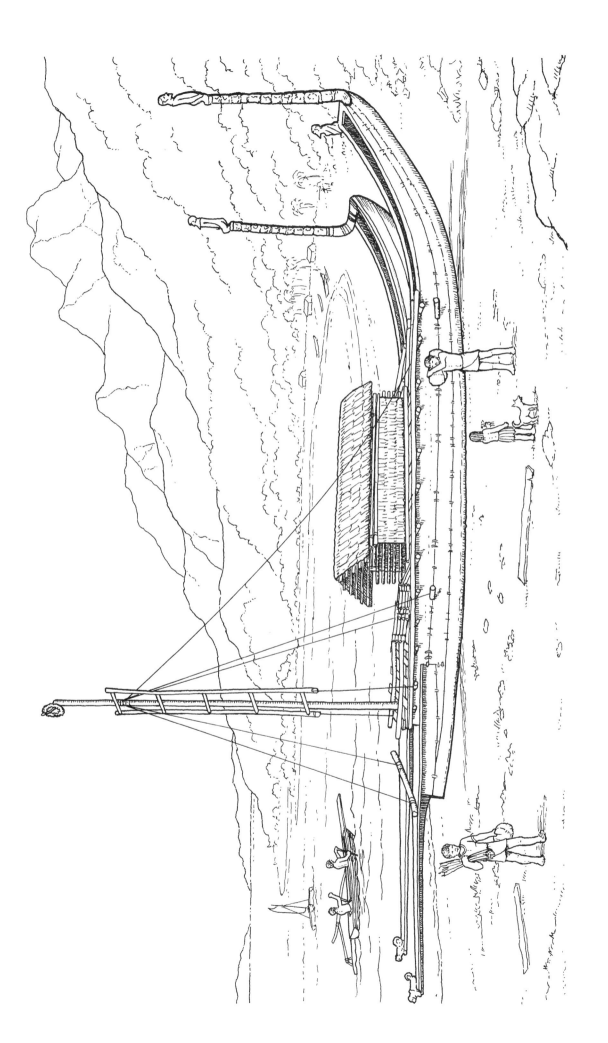

26. A large oceangoing Polynesian double canoe, Tahiti. The length of the hulls is 60 feet; overall length is 90 feet.

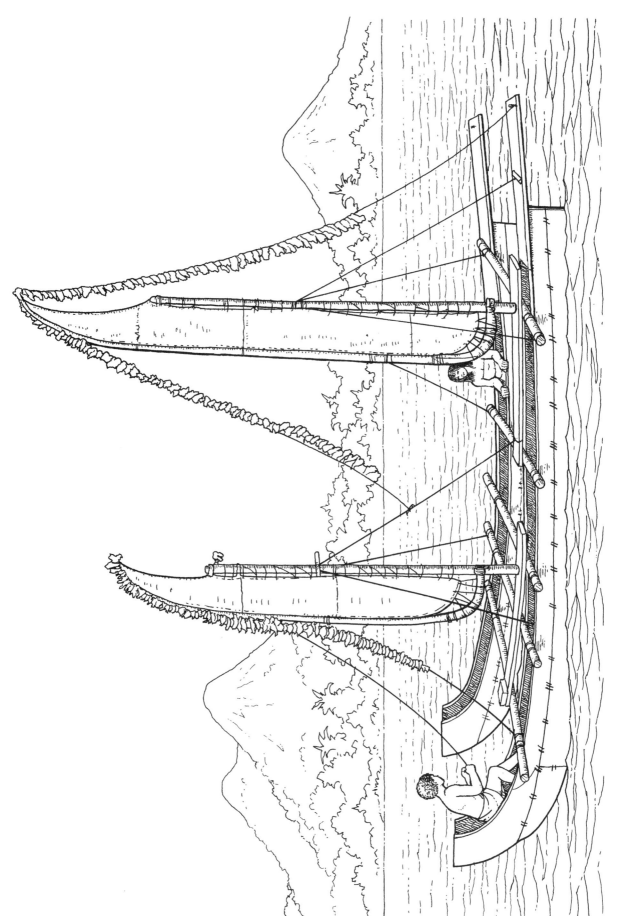

27. A Polynesian double outrigger canoe with twin fore-and-aft masts. The farther from their original Asian homelands the Pacific Islanders migrated, the more the design of their boats' rigging changed.

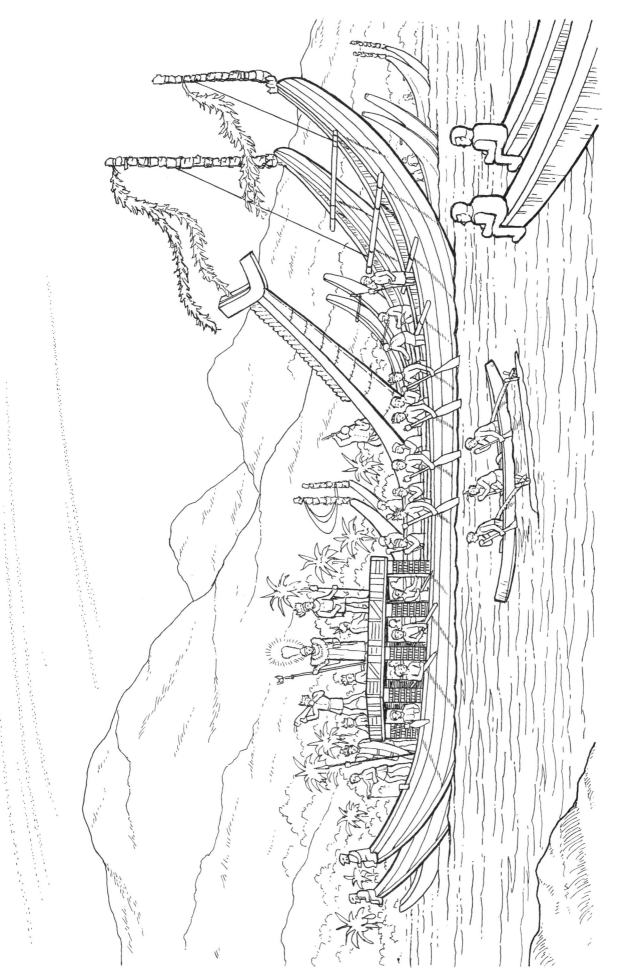

28. A gathering of Tahitian war canoes before a sea battle. These expeditions were preceded by much ritual and ceremony.

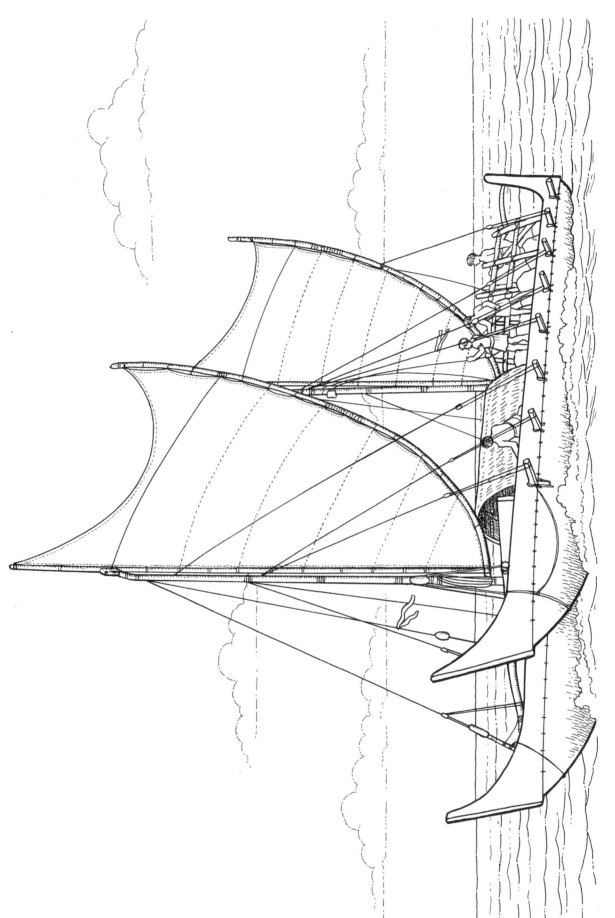

29. A large Hawaiian double-hulled, twin-masted sailing canoe. In the mid-twentieth century, modern sailors looked back to these craft and developed the modern catamaran and trimaran sailboats of today. Their speed surpasses that of modern single-hulled yachts.